SOR JUANA

A TRAILBLAZING THINKER

ELIZABETH COONROD MARTINEZ

Hispanic Heritage
The Millbrook Press
Brookfield, Connecticut

*This painting shows Sor Juana at the front of famous figures in
Mexican history, including Hernando Cortés (far left) the conqueror of Mexico.*

Library of Congress Cataloging-in-Publication Data
Martinez, Elizabeth Coonrod, 1954–
Sor Juana, a trailblazing thinker
by Elizabeth Coonrod Martinez.
p.   cm.—(Hispanic heritage)
Includes bibliographical references and index.
Summary: A biography of the seventeenth-century Mexican nun who
not only wrote poetry and plays and conducted botanical studies but
was world famous for her knowledge of many subjects.
ISBN 1-56294-406-1 (lib. bdg.)
1. Juana Inés de la Cruz, Sister, 1651–1695—Biography—Juvenile
literature.   2. Authors, Mexican—17th century—Biography—Juvenile
literature.   3. Nuns—Mexico—Biography—Juvenile literature.
[1. Juana Inés de la Cruz, Sister, 1651–1695.   2. Authors, Mexican.
3. Nuns.]   I. Title.   II. Series.
PQ7296.J6Z6955   1994
861—dc20   [B]   93-15095   CIP   AC

Cover photograph courtesy of
Michael Calderwood/AMI/Art Resource, New York

Photographs courtesy of Museo Nacional de Arqueologia, Historia
y Etnografia, reprinted from *Anales 1934:* pp. 3, 23; Bettmann:
p. 4; reprinted from *La Ruta de Sor Juana:* pp. 7, 19, 29;
Superstock: p. 8; New York Public Library Picture Collection:
pp. 10, 27; Culver Pictures: pp. 11, 25; Laurie Platt Winfrey:
pp. 12, 21; Peter Arnold, Inc.: p. 14 (© Estate of D. Mooshake);
Bob Schalkwijk/AMI/Art Resource, New York: p. 16; Alinavi
Art Resource, New York: p. 22.

Published by The Millbrook Press
2 Old New Milford Road, Brookfield, Connecticut 06804

SOR JUANA

The University of Mexico City's library as it looks today. A mural by Mexican painter Juan O'Gorman decorates the outside.

Juana was six years old when she first heard about the University of Mexico City. The university, Juana discovered, was the largest place of learning in the country where she lived, Mexico. It had a library containing thousands of books. The people who went to the university could study art, science, history, and many other subjects.

The more Juana thought about the university, the more she yearned to go there someday. Although Juana was still very young, she loved books and studying. She knew how to read by the age of three. Juana lived in her grandfather's house, and one of her favorite things to do was to sneak into his library and spend hours reading his books. Her grandfather punished her for this, because he thought she was too young to read and would ruin his books. Juana thought that if she could attend the university, she could read all the books she wanted, go to classes, and, most of all, learn.

Juana announced her plan to go to the university to her mother. Juana's mother told her that only men could go there. What if she dressed up like a boy, Juana offered, *then* would she be allowed to go? Juana's mother replied: no. Girls and women did not go to school; only boys and men did. That was all.

But, for Juana, that was not all. She vowed to keep alive her love of learning. In Juana's time, the 1600s, there was only one way a woman could do this—by becoming a nun. So when Juana reached the age of nineteen, she joined a group of nuns in the Roman Catholic Church. She moved into a convent—a place where nuns live—and changed her name to Sor Juana Ines de la Cruz. *Sor* means "Sister," and *de la Cruz* means "of the Cross."

Juana achieved her goal—and went far beyond it. How did this young girl who wanted to know about everything become one of her country's greatest writers and thinkers of all time? In an era when women had few rights and most women could not read, how did Juana manage to write books that are still read today?

A YOUNG LOVER OF BOOKS · Sor Juana's full name was Juana Ines de Asbaje y Ramirez. She was born near Mexico City in a country village called San Miguel de Nepantla. The date was November 12, 1648.

Juana's little village was quiet and peaceful, with farms and wide dirt roads she could walk along with her two older sisters. Alongside her village ran a lovely river,

*The Catholic church at San Miguel de Nepantla,
Juana's home town.*

where Juana could sit and look up at the mountains. In the mountains were two of Mexico's largest volcanoes. The Aztecs, the Native Americans who lived in that area before the Spaniards came, named them Popocatepetl and Ixtaccihuatl. The bigger of the two volcanoes was nick-named "Popo." Juana often watched the little puff of smoke coming out of Popo's top. Someday she would learn what caused that puff of smoke, she decided.

Beyond rolling green hills—the mighty Popo.

Trees and wildflowers also grew near the river, and Juana liked to look at those, too. When she got older, Juana would study flowers and make scientific experiments on them. But right now she just liked to gaze at their colors while lying on the soft green grass.

Juana's father did not live with her mother, so she never got to know him. However, Juana, her mother, and her two sisters lived at her grandfather's big ranch.

When Juana was about three years old, her sisters started going to school and left her to play with the house servants' children, who also lived at the ranch. Juana wasn't really interested in playing. She was more curious about what her sisters were doing at school. She begged to go with them, but her mother told her she was too young. Juana, however, was determined. When her sisters came home from school, she asked them to show her their books and tell her what the words in them said. But they didn't really know how to teach her.

So Juana got an idea. She followed her sisters to school one day and told the reading teacher that her mother had sent her to learn to read. Even though the teacher knew that was a lie, she was impressed with this little three-year-old. She decided to go ahead and teach Juana. When Juana had learned the letters of the alphabet and how to read words, the teacher let her read some simple books. Juana felt powerful. She could read things!

Juana's mother eventually found out she had been visiting the teacher. The teacher encouraged Juana's mother to let her keep coming, since she learned so quickly. Juana's mother still thought she was too young to read and said no.

This didn't stop Juana. Even though she couldn't attend school, she kept sneaking into the library at home and reading more and more books. She read about everything she was curious about; she didn't want any-

A Mexican girl reads on a hill far away from town in this woodcut. Like her, young Juana read often alone and in secret.

thing to stop her from learning. One day she heard from someone in the village that eating cheese might make your mind dull. From that day on, Juana wouldn't eat any cheese because she wanted only to be smart. Later, when she was grown up, she learned that the cheese story was not true.

LIFE IN THE CITY · When Juana turned ten years old, her mother thought she was old enough to live in Mexico City. There she could eventually get a job teaching or taking care of children, or find a husband when she got a little older. So Juana's mother decided to send her to live with her aunt and uncle in the city. Juana was so excited she could hardly sleep. She thought of the people she would meet; there would be people to exchange ideas with in the *plazas,* the town squares, where people got together to talk. And there would be many sights to see. Mexico City was beautiful back then because it had canals and waterways running through it. Instead of walking or riding in horse-drawn carriages, people often took rowboats in these canals to get from one part of the city to another.

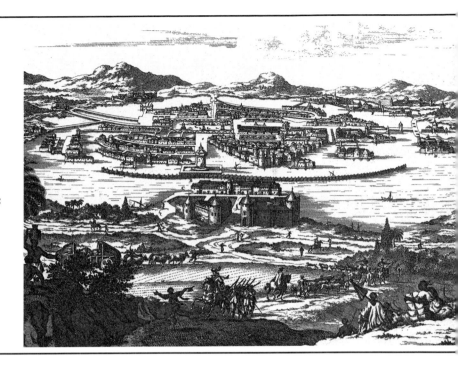

Mexico City as it looked in Juana's time. The city was built on an island in the middle of Lake Texcoco and was connected to land by bridges. Eventually the lake was drained.

When Juana arrived in Mexico City, she found it was all she had imagined. That was until she laid eyes on the university. From the inside of her horse-drawn carriage, she saw it. It had ancient stone buildings where men in long black robes walked. It looked like a place full of wisdom. And Juana knew she would never be allowed to go inside this place of learning—all because she was a girl!

Juana's aunt and uncle did, however, hire a tutor, or private teacher, for her. That was how many girls were

Aztec writing consisted of small pictures called pictographs. These pictographs tell of Tonatiuh (center), the sun god.

taught in Juana's time, if they were taught at all. Her tutor was a specialist in Latin. Juana soon had a perfect knowledge of the ancient language. Then she learned Nahuatl, the language that the Aztecs, the Native Americans of Mexico City, spoke. She also studied Portuguese and Basque, which was her grandfather's native language and was very difficult.

Juana learned these languages fast because she asked her tutor for a very strict study schedule. She also decided to cut off all her long hair, vowing to keep cutting it off if she did not learn as fast as she wanted to. In those days, girls and women did not cut their hair. Long hair was their sign of beauty. But Juana decided that if she didn't have the beauty of wisdom, she would not allow herself to have beautiful hair.

Juana's tutor admired her because she was so smart and so dedicated to learning. She admired him, too, because he helped her achieve her goals. But at one point there was no more he could teach her. She had learned everything *he* knew. After that, Juana continued to study, but by herself.

BECOMING A POET AND PLAYWRIGHT · By this time, Juana had started writing poetry. Sometimes she showed her poems to the priests at the local church, and they liked them very much. The priests decided to print Juana's poems in a church newspaper. She even won a prize for one of her religious poems. It was the best prize of all: a book! Juana decided to keep writing poems.

Juana attended the Catholic church faithfully with her relatives. She had a confessor whom she talked to once a week. A confessor is a priest a Catholic talks to in a private booth in church. The Catholic tells him the bad things he or she has done, and then receives the confessor's blessing and forgiveness.

SOR JUANA'S POETRY

Sor Juana Ines de la Cruz wrote thousands of poems. In this one she compares people to a rose. In the beginning of the poem the rose seems so perfect and beautiful, it's as if it might live forever and never grow old. People, by comparison, seem only to age and lose their beauty. Is the rose greater because of this? Juana considers this question in the poem. By the end she points out that the rose's beauty isn't what it seems.

ROSE TELLS THE TRUTH

Gentle rose, rose divine,
With soft fragrance
And solemn grace,
In your beauty lessons lie.

So elegant, so blest,
You make us ashamed;
From cradle to grave,
We can only be second best.

High on your stem,
Unafraid of death
Till you wither and fade
and then

With your last breath,
There's a truth you tell:
You had us fooled oh so well!

Juana's confessor was also the confessor of people from Spain who ruled Mexico. Mexico was not an independent country at the time Juana lived. It was a colony, or territory, belonging to Spain. Spain's king, Charles II, set up a palace in Mexico City. He sent some of his family members to rule Mexico from this palace. These people were called viceroyals. They tried to imitate the royal court in Spain, and wanted to surround themselves with beautiful and smart people.

Juana's confessor told some of the viceroyals about this smart teenage girl, and what a fine poet she was. The viceroyals wanted to meet her.

Juana was summoned to the royal palace. There the viceroyals had her talk to them about many different subjects: science, literature, art, and even medicine. They were deeply impressed with her knowledge. The viceroyals decided to have Juana tested by experts. They invited forty professors from the university to come and ask Juana questions. No matter what subject they asked her about, she answered everything perfectly! These men thought this fifteen-year-old girl was the smartest student they had ever seen. The viceroyals then offered Juana a job. They asked her to be an assistant, or helper, to a viceroyal's wife. That meant Juana would read to her, keep her company, and write letters and poems for her.

Juana accepted the job—and took her duties a step further. Pretty soon she started writing plays, too. She

This painting shows gardens in Mexico City's center, called the Zocalo. As a member of the royal palace, Juana could study plants in these and other gardens.

wrote plays on request from people in the palace, and they were performed before audiences.

The best part about living and working in the royal palace was that Juana could learn, just as if she had gone to the university. Juana could read all the books the palace received from Europe. Often she received books as presents. She learned about the latest art and music in

Europe. Juana also learned to paint. She would paint miniature pictures, which she gave as gifts to the viceroyals. The palace had gardens and patios. Here Juana could examine flowers and plants that she had read about.

Juana was expanding and refining her knowledge in what was then one of the liveliest civilizations in the Americas. In North America, people were still only getting settled at Jamestown, and it was more than a hundred years before the United States became a country.

BECOMING A NUN · Juana enjoyed the time she spent working at the palace, but she wanted to do something more with her life. She wanted to write things that were more meaningful than the things she wrote to entertain the viceroyals. About three blocks from the palace was a convent. Juana admired the work the nuns who lived there did, like teaching and taking care of people. When she was almost nineteen years old, she decided to join this convent and become a nun herself.

Juana worked very hard at being a nun. After only three months she worked so hard that she became very ill and had to leave the convent. She returned to live with her aunt and uncle again and thought about her future.

In her time, Juana didn't have a lot of choices. She could either get married or try to be a nun again. Juana knew she could not get married to one of the young men she met in the royal palace because she had no dowry. A dowry is a sum of money that a bride brings into a marriage. Juana was poor and did not have a father, who usually provides the dowry. No rich man would marry a young woman without a large dowry. Juana knew that if she married a poor man she would not have an opportunity to read and study. She would have to work all of the time. So Juana decided that, instead of marriage, she would dedicate her life to her studies. The only way she could do that was to become a member of a convent that allowed her to study.

When Juana was healthy and strong again, she joined the Convent of the Order of Saint Jerome. To be in this convent, Juana had to pay a dowry. (The word *dowry* is also used to describe this kind of payment.) Since Juana didn't have any money, a rich man helped her. He liked to support young men and women who wanted to become priests and nuns. Because of his help, Juana could be in a convent where she didn't have to scrub floors and cook. Her job in the convent was to read and study, and write things that people asked her to write. She brought all her books from the palace and continued to order more until she soon had a library of thousands of books, as large as her grandfather's.

She also had her own room. This convent was located on the outskirts of the city, and from the window of her upstairs room Juana could see the mountains and the two volcanoes, Popocatepetl and Ixtaccihuatl. She kept writing poems and plays for the people in the royal palace, but she also wrote poems and plays for the Catholic Church. Juana developed a great love of writing.

The church of Saint Jerome. Next door was the convent where Juana lived.

BECOMING FAMOUS · The nuns were not allowed to go outside the walls of the convent. It was like a huge castle with many gardens and patios. They could have visitors, however. Many people came from the royal palace to visit Juana and have conversations with her. Sometimes new people, like scientists and travelers from Europe, came to Juana's private room and asked her opinions on many subjects. Some of her friends were even university professors. Juana was very entertaining because she had a delightful personality. She would make up poems at the very moment someone was talking to her, or she might play word games with her visitors. She could also talk in different languages to them. Word of her quick wit soon spread.

Juana also read and studied science in the convent and sometimes experimented with combining, or breeding, certain types of plants with others. She kept scientific instruments in her room. She even made a study of all the different plants of Mexico. She painted their pictures in notebooks and wrote down what she learned about the plants.

Juana also did experiments in the kitchen. She tried new combinations of foods and wrote about her discoveries. Juana was a reader of the ancient Greek philosophers, the greatest thinkers of all time. But she decided they knew nothing of some of the wonders of the kitchen:

*Sor Juana
Ines de
la Cruz in
her study.*

that an egg stays together and cooks in oil, but separates into many pieces in syrup; and that melted sugar will remain liquid if a little lemon water is added to it. These discoveries made Juana think: If the great Greek philosopher Aristotle had cooked, how much more he would have known and told us about!

Juana also collected musical instruments and could play them well. She set many of her poems to music and entertained her visitors and the other nuns. Some of these poems were used in the schools in Mexico City to teach young boys.

Juana collected and played musical instruments such as the ones shown in this painting by German artist Hans Holbein the Younger.

Many of the poems and songs and plays that Juana wrote in the twenty-seven years she was in this convent made her very well known, especially in Europe. During her lifetime two volumes of her writings were published because of her friends' help.

Juana continued to write anything the viceroyals and the religious leaders asked her to write. Some of the things she wrote, however, worried the Church leaders. They didn't want a woman explaining scientific things that only men in the Church were allowed to explain. Juana's confessor, who had

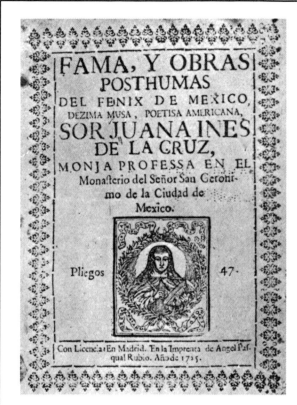

A page from an early book of Juana's writings published in Spain.

introduced her to the viceroyals, was also a member of the Spanish Inquisition. He warned her several times to "behave" and not write so much. But Juana paid no attention to him. She also had powerful friends who were Church members.

THE SPANISH INQUISITION

The *Spanish Inquisition* was established in 1478 by King Ferdinand and Queen Isabella of Spain. They were trying to unite their country, which had people of several religions living in it. There were Roman Catholics, Moors (people from North Africa who practiced the religion of Islam), and Jews. The king and queen, who were Catholics, thought Spain would be stronger if it had only one religion, Roman Catholicism. The Inquisition was an organization set up in the Catholic Church to make the religion more powerful. Sometimes this involved punishing people—and even torturing and killing them—if they were believed to be enemies of the Church. The Inquisition took property away from Jews and Moors, and helped run them out of Spain.

By the 1600s, when Spain ruled most of Latin America, the men who worked for the Inquisition came to Mexico and other parts of the Americas to interview and punish people for not doing what the Catholic Church wanted them to do. They didn't want people to do anything on their own, but only obey the orders the Church gave. They didn't want people to think and have new ideas, as Sor Juana did.

The Inquisition lost its power as Spain started losing its world power in the 1800s. It officially ended in 1843, but not before it had done much to harm people whose views it did not like.

The Spanish Inquisition often tortured those accused of crimes, like the man in this painting. Such people often confessed to the crimes whether they were guilty or not.

MAKING THE CHURCH ANGRY · One day a bishop of the city of Puebla asked her to write an essay criticizing a famous sermon. The bishop knew the essay would make his boss, the archbishop, angry because the archbishop admired the person who had written the sermon. Juana didn't know when she wrote her interesting essay that the bishop would publish it and the archbishop would read it.

The archbishop was indeed angry when he read her essay, but he got even angrier when Juana wrote a letter three months later explaining why she wrote what she did. This letter was published, too.

In her letter, Juana wrote that women should be able to study, think, and write. This upset the archbishop. He didn't want to have to read things women wrote. The archbishop had a lot of power, and he told the convent not to let Sor Juana write anything else. She had to give up her fight to study and write because the archbishop was more powerful than her friends in Mexico City. Most of her friends at the royal palace had died or moved back to Europe, and they could not protect her. Meanwhile, her confessor also threatened her with the Inquisition.

Juana stopped writing at about the same time Mexico City came upon hard times. There was a terrible shortage of food, a famine, and many people did not have enough to eat. The convent didn't receive as many donations, and it became poor. Juana was forced to sell her wonderful library of books, along with her collection of musical and mathematical instruments. She felt very sad and no longer talked to visitors or her friends from the royal palace. She dedicated herself to helping people who were sick.

In this woodcut men carry a victim of the plague that struck Mexico City in Juana's time. At the plague's height more than 500 people died each day.

A plague also struck Mexico City. In Juana's convent many of her sister nuns got sick and died. After a year of caring for nuns and others who were sick, Juana began to grow weak and tired. Finally, she got sick herself.

Juana knew she was dying. She was forty-seven years old, and it had been four years since she wrote her last item, the letter to the bishop. Juana thought about writing one last poem, but she knew it was too late. The greatest Mexican woman poet and thinker had put away her pen and books forever. She died on the night of April 17, 1695.

Although it has been three hundred years since her death, Juana's people remember her well. The village where she was born, San Miguel de Nepantla, has been renamed Nepantla de Sor Juana Ines de la Cruz. The new name means "Sister Juana's Nepantla." A piece of the wall of the room where she was born still stands, and it is now a monument with a fence around it. Beautiful gardens surround this monument, and a visitor standing beside it can see the "Popo" volcano that fascinated Juana. Nearby, there's an open-air theater, which is named Sor Juana Theater. From here, visitors can see some of the same wildflowers and trees and the river that inspired Juana when she was a little girl just starting to read and think.

The remaining wall of Juana's house at Nepantla
de Sor Juana de la Cruz.

IMPORTANT DATES
IN THE LIFE OF
SOR JUANA INES DE LA CRUZ

1648	Juana is born on November 16 in San Miguel de Nepantla.
1658	Juana moves to Mexico City to live with her aunt and uncle.
1663	Juana goes to work for the royal palace.
1667	Juana joins her first convent, but leaves after she becomes very ill.
1669	Juana joins the Convent of the Order of Saint Jerome.
1691	Sor Juana's essay makes the archbishop angry.
1695	Sor Juana dies on April 17.

FIND OUT MORE
ABOUT
SOR JUANA INES DE LA CRUZ

Sor Juana Ines de la Cruz. Milwaukee, Wis.: Raintree, 1990.

FIND OUT MORE
ABOUT MEXICO

Count Your Way Through Mexico by Jim Haskins. Minneapolis: Carolrhoda, 1989.

Mexico by Sam and Beryl Epstein. New York: Franklin Watts, 1983.

Mexico by Ian James. New York: Franklin Watts, 1990.

Take a Trip to Mexico by Keith Lye. New York: Franklin Watts, 1982.

INDEX